MANAGING DIFFERENCES
A Guide to Proactive Management Skills

by Geri McArdle, Ph.D.

MANAGING DIFFERENCES
A Guide to Proactive Management Skills

Geri McArdle, Ph.D.

CREDITS
Editor: Bev Manber
Design: ExecuStaff
Typesetting: ExecuStaff
Cover Artwork: David Smith/Carol Harris

Copyright © 1995 by Crisp Publications, Inc.

Library of Congress Catalog Card Number 93-74234
McArdle, Geri
Managing Differences
ISBN 1-56052-320-4

This book is printed on recyclable paper with soy ink

CONTENTS

INTRODUCTION

Have you ever found yourself in a difficult situation that ultimately resulted in a heated debate, filled with over-charged emotions evolving around different points of view? At the time, did the situation seem impossible to resolve even though you were certain that the keys to resolving the differences were within everyone's grasp? Guess what? If you answered "yes," you're not alone!

Differences stem from a myriad of sources. You may be presented with differences in the workplace, you may become embroiled in disputes regarding race, religion, education, gender or sexual orientation. Differences can also arise during a decision-making process—differences that are based on management and/or organizational styles, maturity levels, and struggles for power or dominance. The keys to a successful outcome are understanding how differences can manifest themselves in any given situation, and preparing yourself for them so they don't escalate into an unmanageable conflict.

In fact, by learning to view differences as signals that indicate when a difficult situation is brewing, you may give yourself time to reframe the situation and even use the differences between people or groups to create valuable alternative solutions to a commonly held problem. In doing so, you will enable yourself to manage the differences proactively, before a crisis occurs.

Some differences can easily be brought to a win-win resolution, in which everyone walks away fulfilled. More often, however, without the skills for managing differences, the parties involved find themselves ensnared in power struggles that are rooted in attitude and perceptions of behavior, or simply faced with divergent opinions on the disputed issues.

This book discusses some of the wide range of factors that come into play when we attempt to manage differences. You can expect to acquire an understanding of the factors motivating individuals when they encounter differences—differences that ultimately result in conflict. You will gain insights into effectively managing these types of disputes. And you will be able to apply these tools to everyday situations at work, at home and in social settings.

After reading this book, answering the questions and working through the exercises it contains, you will never again have to walk away from a confrontational situation feeling that you were unable to air your differences constructively. The negotiation and persuasion techniques described in this book will help you resolve differences in an effective manner, enabling you to feel like a winner—and to make everyone else feel the same way, too!

SECTION ONE

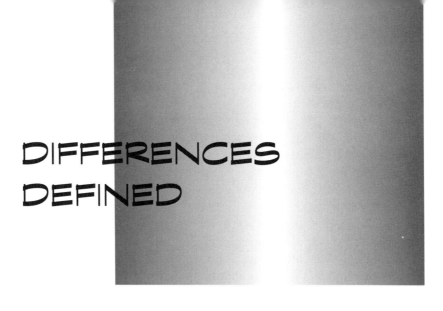

DIFFERENCES DEFINED

Differences can become apparent and a source of conflict when people struggle as they share their preferences, ideas, perceptions or goals. Whether at home or at work, you invariably encounter people who hold views and act in ways that differ from your own routines. These differences highlight approaches to problem solving that may not be compatible.

Some differences do not disturb the status quo. Others, of greater magnitude, can create constant tension or enmity at home or in the workplace.

The ability to resolve successfully conflicts that result from our differences is probably one of the most important social skills you can possess. Yet, our society provides few opportunities in which you can easily learn how to manage and handle differences.

As the workforce becomes increasingly diverse, human resource professionals are among those who are painfully aware of both our need to deal effectively with differences and the limited examples of skillful leadership that are available. With an ever-increasing number of special interest populations contending for the same opportunities, it is no longer feasible politely to ignore the differences.

Traditionally, we took time to manage differences that caused conflict. The relationship between differences and conflict is still important and one that we will explore. However, in today's hyper-speed world proactive strategies are now required. Waiting for a conflict to develop is, as Grandpa used to say, like locking the barn door *after* the cow was stolen. While conflict can be productive, it is costly and time consuming.

To manage differences, you must first understand how *you* feel about them. Our natural inclination is to assume that our way is the best way. You may have fixed thoughts, perceptions or attitudes about differences, which influence the role you play when a difference arises. You must see differences as part of the on-going process of organizational growth and development. Differences are not independent entities that need to be snuffed out like little brush fires. Rather, they are the components, or even subcomponents, that fuel the engine of change.

Differences become apparent when values, priorities and goals seem incompatible. Such differences are frequently based on an individual's perceptions, rather than on reality. The following graphic illustrates the major factors that interact in the management of differences.

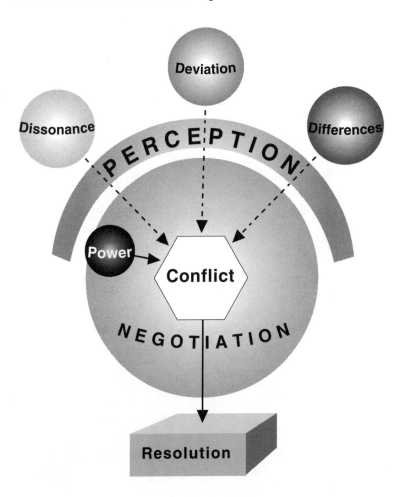

PERCEPTION VERSUS REALITY

Most of us consistently seek and establish predictable behavior patterns. These behavioral patterns build connecting webs between and among other people, places and things; the interconnection helps each of us make sense of every-day experiences.

Your reactions and how you interact with others is based upon the way in which you perceive the world around you, and your interpretation of reality provides you with a unique viewpoint. Every day, you interpret events and use a system of beliefs based on your background and experiences. Your beliefs support your reality and create meaning out of otherwise random events, while they influence your thoughts, actions and reactions. You also access folk wisdom (stories or truisms) passed down through your family, and personal theories that help to guide your reality.

ATTITUDE VERSUS BEHAVIOR

Attitude and behavior are also profoundly influenced by your perception of reality. Attitude, the individual's habitual outlook on the world, significantly determines how that person chooses to conduct him or herself in given situations, including those characterized by differences of opinion. That is, attitude guides behavior. Behavior is the way in which the individual chooses to conduct him or herself—both at home and in the workplace.

As humans, we are motivated by needs. These needs are the under-lying motives for the majority of our behaviors. Some of these needs we act on, others we don't. What motivates you to take action?

Some social scientists contend that when a need is satisfied, it no longer motivates behavior. Also, some needs can take precedence and become all-encompassing, inciting a person to take action. The obstruction of needs leads an individual to various coping mechanisms.

One rational way to cope with differences is to attempt to overcome potential obstacles to needs—by trial and error, or by problem solving. For example, you may try to adopt a variety of behaviors until you find a behavior that ultimately leads you to attain your needs or goals or to resolve the differences you face.

DIFFERENCES, DEVIATION AND COGNITIVE DISSONANCE

You may have noticed that the route you need to take to satisfy your needs sometimes leads to further differences, deviation and cognitive dissonance. Every member of society has a specific viewpoint. Our varying viewpoints in turn create a world of differences, which we need to respect. Some differences, for example, follow definite patterns and are not typically associated with angry feelings; other differences, as you will soon learn, involve irrational behavior and lead to disruptive and even violent actions.

All differences and differing viewpoints radiate from some agreed upon standard or norm of behavior. Deviations, however, account for differences that appear occasionally, which are inconsistent with one of society's established behavioral norms. Obstructed motives and unsuccessful attempts to resolve interpersonal issues may surface when a person behaves irrationally in an uncomfortable situation. Their irrational behavior may be evidence of what is known as *cognitive dissonance.*

This term describes times when it becomes difficult or impossible for an individual to reconcile perceptions and conditions of his or her environment. The individual may notice feelings of tension or anxiety. While conflicting feelings are part of an internal process that others may not notice, the feelings may result in behavior others find confusing.

Cognitive dissonance can also arise when two people who meet or work together have dramatically different perceptions of an issue. The collision of incompatible views creates tension that ultimately must be resolved by modifying one viewpoint.

We modify our views or change our behaviors to reduce tension (i.e., dissonance) that develops; we make compromises (under the auspices of coping) to achieve what we perceive to be balanced relationships.

If, for example, an advertising account executive is assigned to a project she detests, the executive might remark that she enjoys being placed on a campaign where she will work with team members whom she enjoys. In this way, that account executive may rid herself of dissonance by focusing on the personalities involved (i.e., the team members). Alternatively, the individual could be appeased by the team members she will work with, while still harboring feelings of dissonance over her new assignment.

The latter example illustrates the frustration and irrational coping behaviors that often result from dissonant feelings. Ultimately, this dissonance can lead to aggression and hostility, which can diminish job productivity. In the worst-case scenario, this type of hostility can lead to destructive behavior if the individual acts out his or her aggressions. In those situations, the person directs his or her hostility against the person or object that he or she feels is the source of the frustration.

An angry worker, for example, may resort to retaliatory actions such as gossiping, undermining the boss, sabotaging a project (and simultaneously his or her job) or acting out other kinds of malicious behavior. Subconsciously, that person may look for a scapegoat as a target for the hostility. Unfortunately, innocent colleagues, family members or friends become the victims and bear the brunt of such aggressive behavior.

In contrast, people who know how to cope well with dissonance may behave in a more constructive manner (e.g., going to the gym, running or engaging in some other kind of physical activity). In this way, they redirect their focus harmlessly away from the person(s) or subject(s) of the differences.

Recognize that not all differences, deviations and feelings of dissonance are negative experiences. Similarly, not all differences result in a conflict. Differences become potential sources of conflict or distress only when they are not properly addressed.

QUICK
SELF
APPRAISAL

Have you ever experienced differences that centered around one or more of the following issues?

1. Pressure to meet deadlines

2. Personal differences

3. Distribution of resources

4. Authority

5. Seniority

6. Dispute settlement

7. Affirmative action

8. Interdepartmental concerns

9. Use of human resources

10. Giving and receiving information

Don't judge yourself harshly if you answered "yes" to any of these questions. Instead, ask yourself why the differences reached the point they did. Take the opportunity to learn how you can deal with differences and take control of your options now.

DIFFERENCES, DISAGREEMENT AND CONFLICT

Differences can evolve into disagreements, which can ultimately result in three types of conflict: overt, escalated and covert.

Overt conflict involves open, adversarial interaction. This interaction can range from mild disagreement to high-level disagreement that results in fighting. Labor-management disputes that make headlines are typical examples of overt conflict.

Escalated conflict occurs when groups with different levels of power enter into a disagreement. An example of this can be seen in an intergroup meeting between a low-power group and a high-power group. Perceiving their vulnerability, the low-power group may feel forced to withhold information from the high-power group; without the information, the high-power group would be unaware that the low-power group is dissatisfied with specific issues. Over time, the low-power group would continue to repress information to avoid repercussions. Such differences are harmful; they deny opportunities to discuss and resolve the problem, and to work toward positive, valuable solutions.

Covert conflict often involves societal differences such as gender, race and religious discrimination. These differences are highly sensitive and must be handled with extra care and consideration. Laws and business regulations that guarantee equal opportunity can do little to change deep-seated attitudes and behaviors.

Consequently, interpersonal differences can turn into conflict unless a catalyst—an unbiased person or set of circumstances—successfully motivates a discussion where differences can be aired openly and freely.

ATTITUDE
QUESTIONNAIRE

Directions: To help you identify your basic beliefs about differences, look at these ten commonly held beliefs about differing viewpoints. Read each statement carefully. Indicate how you feel about the statement; mark a plus for *agree* and a minus for *disagree.*

_____ **1.** Once I get wound up in a heated discussion about differences, I just can't stop.

_____ **2.** If people communicated more there would be fewer differences.

_____ **3.** There is always a winner and a loser when matters of difference are expressed.

_____ **4.** Differing viewpoints are something I want to get rid of.

_____ **5.** When I'm upset, I shouldn't discuss my differences about important issues.

_____ **6.** Differences in viewpoints make me feel uneasy and anxious.

_____ **7.** I like to win when differences present a challenge.

_____ **8.** It is difficult for me to discuss my feelings when I might have a difference with colleagues, friends or family members.

_____ **9.** I seldom can think straight when my opinions are different from others.

_____ **10.** Resolving differences has provided great opportunities for my personal growth.

Attitude Questionnaire Key

Since your answers are based on your attitudes, there are no right or wrong answers to this questionnaire. It goes without saying that you're entitled to your feelings, attitudes and beliefs. The following suggestions will help you understand your answers:

1. Most of us have difficulty thinking straight during a heated discussion. Yet, it is important that we take time to think through our responses. Picture yourself in the other person's shoes: What is he or she thinking, feeling, sensing, hearing and believing? Get a different perspective.

2. Do more listening than talking. You can't think and talk at the same time. This is especially true when you try to understand another's point of view to resolve differences.

3. Differences of opinion don't have to become win/lose situations. Consider redefining the issues by noting points of compatibility or congruity, so that you and the other party improve your opportunities to reach amenable terms, and you *both* can win.

4. You'll never be able to wish away your differences; learn to deal with them. Remember—wishes come true—not free!

5. Oh, yes, you should discuss it! Silence does not make problems go away. The "silent treatment" does not help the other person understand your differences. Talking will help get things moving. Take the risk!

6. It's normal to feel uneasy. Be bold—dare to take charge!

7. Winning is not the goal—it's how skillfully you manage the differences.

8. In matters of difference, emotions make communicating difficult for everyone involved. It is hard to express yourself clearly and to listen with an open mind.

9. Sometimes you lose your thoughts. When it happens, stop and ask for clarification of the issue or problem. Determine your own needs and identify those of the other party. Use the new information as the key to rephrase your dialogue, to unlock the doors to your differences.

10. We often hear that problems create opportunities. When you encounter a problem, take time out and think about at least one alternative way to resolve your differences. You'll be surprised at the flexibility you can exercise!

SUMMARY

Differences in attitudes, perceptions and behaviors can result in conflict. And when differences become disagreements, overt, escalated and covert conflict can evolve.

These three types of conflict couldn't occur, however, without one key ingredient: *power*. As you'll learn in Section Two, power is the underlying issue in the majority of conflicts based on differences that we must handle. It is the driving force in many adversarial situations. You will see that power is a multidimensional agent, derived from various bases and sources. It plays a number of roles in matters where differences are at issue.

SECTION TWO

POWER BASES
AND DIFFERENCES

Power has many definitions. At the simplest level, power is the ability to do or to affect something or someone. Handled wisely at an organizational level, power can inspire actions that set a good example for others to follow, and provide the leadership and inspiration that prevent differences from becoming destructive conflicts. In a sense, it is like electricity, which, when harnessed and applied skillfully, allows us to heat our homes, cook our food and provide light in the darkness.

While it can be deadly when misused, power is neither inherently good or bad. In sum, power is an individual's potential to influence.

THE RELATIONSHIP BETWEEN
POWER AND CONFLICT

Power is the underlying issue that drives most situations of conflict that focus on differences. Differences that have the potential to escalate into a destructive conflict usually involve the issue of power. One party has power, while another doesn't have it; one party feels abused, doesn't know to wield power, doesn't want power or wishes to have more power.

Differences can lead to struggles and useless conflict about power—both with others and with oneself. In a variety of situations, understanding power is the key to managing behavior and productively resolving differences.

POSITIONAL VERSUS PERSONAL POWER

Power takes on two forms: positional and personal. An individual who induces compliance from others because of his or her status within an organization has positional power. Influence derived from personality, gender, race, education and behavior is said to have personal power. Some individuals possess both positional and personal power. And, while some individuals possess some power, others possess none at all.

If you are a department manager, you have genuine organizational (i.e., positional) power over your immediate staff. At the same time, you defer to senior management.

Positional and personal power are two important elements related to the way we view differences. Both elements are crucial to understanding what motivates others when differences arise.

POWER-RELATED CONCEPTS

The following basic concepts relate to power:

1. *Power is finite: with respect to resolving differences, it does not have to be perceived in a negative light.*

Although many social scientists maintain that leadership and power form a symbiotic relationship, this is not always the case. To best understand the integral relationship that does exist between the two, you must first understand how power is used.

Power becomes the potential for influence. In this sense, power becomes a valuable resource that you may or may not choose to use when seeking to resolve differences. When power is used to increase the probability that a person or group will adopt a desired behavioral change, this is influence. A distinction can be drawn between leadership and power. Leadership, in the broadest sense, is your attempt to influence another individual, while power is the influence potential of a leader.

If power is defined as potential to influence, how do you distinguish between it and authority? Authority is a distinct type of power that finds its base by default (i.e., the individual's formal role within an organization).

2. Power is the central component of differences.

Power can be a matter of perception. Some differences in power are real, while others are created by perceptions. The chief executive officer of a company has authoritative (i.e., positional) power over a department manager; this is a reality. In another example, because of his gender, one supervisor is perceived by his female colleagues as being more powerful than they. While he may indeed be the only male supervisor in the department, he wields personal power.

3. You have one or more power bases.

We derive power from a variety of sources or bases. Some of these sources lie within the individual (e.g., "I'm more mature than the others"), other power bases are dependent on the individual's position in the organizational hierarchy (e.g., "I'm the department manager now"), his or her expertise (e.g., "I'm more experienced in this area than anyone else") or how others perceive that individual's expertise (e.g., "She sure knows what she's doing; just by watching her management style with her coworkers and subordinates, it's clear why they brought her in to make the department profitable again").

4. Power bases can shift based on matters of difference.

A competent manager can become incompetent if her assistant successfully undermines her authority; in this case, the assistant would be perceived as having more power than the manager. A seasoned (older) assistant may have more power than a newly appointed (younger) manager. If you called a meeting, you may have power because you initiated it.

Remember, we frequently have choices whether or not to use our power bases to effectively and equitably resolve differences.

POWER BASES AND SELF-AWARENESS

Knowing the sources of our power, we can be judicious when we choose to use our power bases. Let's look at seven power bases.

1. *Coercive Power* is based on fear. If you exert coercive power, you can induce compliance through the understanding that the other person's failure to comply will lead to his or her punishment, to retaliation

or, ultimately to dismissal. For the most part, someone exercising coercive power is not concerned with whether his issue is compatible with another person's issue.

2. *Connection Power* is based on an individual's personal and/or professional connection with influential or important people within or outside an organization.

3. *Reward Power* is based on an individual's ability to reward others who believe that they will gain opportunities for growth within an organization (e.g., recognition, pay raise or promotion) by complying now.

4. *Legitimate Power* is based on an individual's authoritative position. The higher their position, the broader others will perceive the scope of their legitimate power. If you have a high degree of legitimate power, you can induce compliance or influence others, simply based upon your position within the organization. In such cases, unfortunately, the subordinates' viewpoints and differences of opinion often go unrecognized and unattended.

5. *Referent Power* is based on personal traits and characteristics. An individual who possesses referent power is generally well-liked and admired by others because of his or her personality.

6. *Information Power* is based on an individual's possession of, or access to, information that is valuable to others. This power base can be very influential when others perceive that they need information that you possess.

7. *Expert Power* is based on education, knowledge, possession of expertise or skills that, through respect, influence others. An individual with expert power is perceived as possessing the expertise required to complete a particular task.

Which type of power base is best for minimizing differences that may arise? In studies conducted by a number of social scientists, expert and referent power achieved the highest levels of satisfactory performance on the job.

Legitimate, reward and coercive power are organizationally determined and designed to be equal for supervisors at a hierarchical level. They are bases for compliance—not satisfaction. Ultimately, your power base and how you choose to resolve differences will be vastly affected by the specific circumstances of each situation.

POWER SOURCES

While some individuals start with little power and gradually build and develop power sources, others gradually allow their power sources to erode. The perception others hold about an individual's power provides that individual with the ability to influence others' behavior, induce compliance or persuade others to agree with a point of view.

STAGES OF POWER

David McClelland, a Harvard psychologist known for his work on individuals' need for achievement, suggests four distinct stages in the development of individual power. Each stage represents a higher level of maturity regarding a person's need for power.

Stage I (Low Maturity Level)   Incorporate power from others. This stage involves incorporating power from a source outside the individual. Early in life, this strength comes from parents, then from friends, a spouse or an admired leader or mentor. By experiencing or sharing the power of a strong person, the individual feels empowered, which leads him or her to believe falsely that anyone can be persuaded easily to abandon his or her differences and "come over to your side."

Stage II (Moderate Maturity Level)   Independent powerfulness. This stage is independent of the self. Usually, when an individual learns self-control, a powerful feeling occurs. This stage is demonstrated by possession of power-associated objects, such as an expensive automobile.

Stage III (Moderate to Rather High Maturity Level)   Power affecting on others. While the primary form of behavior in this stage is competitive, helping behavior is also manifested (i.e., the decision-making process). In accepting help, the receiver can be perceived as acknowledging that he or she is weaker than the person providing the help. Research indicates that many teachers' behavior is predominantly at this stage.

Stage IV (High Maturity Level)   Power derived from a higher authority (i.e., legitimate power) is the final stage in which power is exerted in conformance with duty. At this stage, power is socialized and institutionalized at the highest level. The individual has successfully integrated the three previous stages into the legitimate power, and can use all stages effectively to address and resolve differences that might arise.

CHECK UP

1. What are some examples from your experience of good use of power in resolving differences? Identify what made them so.

   _____

   _____

   _____

   _____

   _____

   _____

   _____

   _____

2. What are some examples from your own experience of bad use of power in resolving differences? Identify what made them so.

   _____

   _____

   _____

   _____

   _____

   _____

   _____

   _____

Now we will examine how power bases can be integrated through the four different maturity levels.

INTEGRATION OF POWER BASES
THROUGH MATURITY LEVELS

The level of maturity of individuals and groups correlates directly to the types of power bases that wield compliance and change the way a given individual or group handles differences.

Here, maturity is viewed as an individual's ability to take responsibility for directing his or her own behavior and resolving differences in a given situation. As that individual moves from lower to higher levels of maturity, his or her confidence and competency levels increase. The seven power bases have a profound impact upon behavior at the various levels of maturity, as well as on an individual's ability to effectively resolve various differences.

Let's explore how maturity levels correspond with the seven different power bases:

1. *Coercive Power* An individual with a low maturity level needs strong directive behavior to be productive. People at low maturity levels are influenced by fear of negative sanctions (e.g., demotion, job threat and dismissal) if they do not play by the rules of the game. At this level, coercive power can be used to motivate or coerce an individual who feels threatened into compliance.

2. *Connection Power* An individual who has reached the next level of maturity, still requires directive behavior but now the influence is accompanied by support. This power base also tends to induce compliance: punishment can be avoided and rewards can be reaped through a powerful connection within or outside of an organization.

3. *Reward Power* At a low to moderate level of maturity, individuals often need great amounts of both directive and supportive behavior. This type of individual exhibits a great sense of willingness and is probably willing to sacrifice personal differences and needs in the hope of being rewarded (either for money, position or some other form of achievement).

4. *Legitimate Power* This power is particularly useful for individuals who have achieved a moderate level of maturity, when compliance can be induced fairly easily. Such individuals can be influenced by someone who exerts positional power within an organizational hierarchy—someone who can induce fear. Ultimately, this fear can lead the individual to completely dismiss any differences.

21

5. *Referent Power* While the individual may have achieved a moderate to rather high level of maturity and requires little direction, he or she still requires a high level of communication and support. This power base is founded on the successful interpersonal relations he or she has established with others. At this stage, the individual feels he or she is a real participant in the process, being involved in decision making and airing differences with others freely. Referent power can be an effective tool in instilling confidence, providing encouragement, support and recognition.

6. *Information Power* An individual who has achieved a higher than average maturity level can use information power as an effective motivational vehicle. At this stage, he or she seeks information on how to maintain or assert skills from the person who wields the power. At this level, the individual can be influenced if the person wielding the power is willing to provide access to necessary information (e.g., data, reports).

7. *Expert Power* An individual who has expert power has achieved a high level of knowledge and maturity. He or she requires little direction or support. While many individuals in an organization have valuable experience, they may still be influenced by an expert.

An individual who has an educational background needed by others and who is willing and able to perform his or her job requirements is viewed as a competent and confident individual. That individual is thought to possess certain expertise and skill. He or she is recognized for his or her merits and achievements. Yet, when differences arise, this same individual can be influenced easily by an individual exerting expert power.

DEVELOPING SOURCES OF POWER

Although the seven power bases can be used to resolve differences, induce compliance or influence the behavior of an individual or group, power can vary greatly. Part of the variance in power is due to the organization for which an individual works and his or her rank within that organization (i.e., position power). The rest of the variance is due to individual differences with other types of power (i.e., personal power). The vehicle with which you choose to resolve a difference in the seven power bases is the key to a productive resolution of differences.

POWER BASE
SELF-AWARENESS

Directions: Think about how you handle power. Work quickly as you jot down one example from your own experience that illustrates how you could use each of the seven sources of power to resolve differences.

1. Coercive Power: _____

_____

2. Legitimate Power: _____

_____

3. Expert Power: _____

_____

4. Reward Power: _____

_____

5. Referent Power: _____

_____

6. Information Power: _____

_____

7. Connection Power: _____

_____

POWER
QUESTIONNAIRE

Directions: Think of a goal you would like to accomplish, which you cannot do unless you resolve differences between yourself and another person, "N." Read the following statements and record how often you would be likely to use the power base described to influence the behavior of another person, so that you could achieve your goal. Use the following scale:

0 = Not at all
1 = Rarely
2 = More often than not
3 = Most of the time

_____ 1. Despite our difference, I want to offer N something I know N wants or values.

_____ 2. I'm in a position to have someone, whose credentials N respects, act on my behalf, to reconcile the differences between N and myself.

_____ 3. I can help N achieve his/her goal, despite our differences.

_____ 4. Using our differences constructively, I can create a situation that would enable me to get what I want from staff.

_____ 5. Despite our differences, I can influence N through my actions.

_____ 6. Because of our differences, I can convince someone else to hurt, punish or deprive N.

_____ 7. By stating our differences clearly, I can make N recognize that we have a lot in common.

_____ 8. Although differences exist, I can drop names that impress N.

_____ 9. I can use my professional knowledge and skills with N, in areas that will help me achieve my goal.

_____ **10.** I can use persuasive techniques to convince N to drop his or her differences.

_____ **11.** To accomplish my goal, I can negate any existing differences by influencing someone else to give N what he or she wants.

_____ **12.** I can use friendship as a means to resolve any differences between N and myself.

_____ **13.** Despite our differences, I can impress N through the people I know.

_____ **14.** I can get a friend of N's to help resolve our differences and to act on my behalf.

_____ **15.** To resolve our differences, I can get someone else who is well connected to influence N.

_____ **16.** I can use N's respect for my education to gain N's support.

_____ **17.** Based on my knowledge in a certain area, I can ask directly for what I want, knowing that N will think it appropriate for me to make the request.

_____ **18.** Recognizing that our differences are being ignored, I can get someone else, who has a legitimate right to ask for something I want, to request what I need from N.

Now, record your answers from your Power Questionnaire on the appropriate lines below.

Formal Power

Reward Power	Coercive Power	Legitimate Power
1. _____	2. _____	3. _____
4. _____	6. _____	17. _____
11. _____	10. _____	18. _____
Total _____	Total _____	Total _____

Informal Power

Expert Power	Referent Power	Associate Power
5. _____	7. _____	8. _____
9. _____	12. _____	13. _____
16. _____	14. _____	15. _____
Total _____	Total _____	Total _____

Total your scores for each power base column. The highest scored category indicates your primary power base; the second scored category indicates your secondary power base.

You'll notice that we've separated out "formal power" bases from "informal power" bases. Formal power bases are seen in more structured situations (e.g., the workplace), where they are more than likely imposed upon the individual. In contrast, the informal power base tends to be less structured and is more likely self-driven.

POWER
PROFILE

Directions: Complete this short description of your power base.

My formal power base for resolving differences:

_____

_____

_____

My informal power base for resolving differences:

_____

_____

_____

The characteristics of both my power bases and the way in which I resolve differences are:

_____

_____

_____

My method for applying my power bases and resolving differences when confronted with differing opinions:

_____

_____

_____

Now, repeat the power profile. This time, respond the way the individual with whom you work closest would answer. After you have completed this exercise, consider asking that individual to complete the profile. Then, compare your answers and note the amount of difference between your perceptions. Keep in mind that each person's perception is that individual's reality and forms the basis of his or her actions.

As you've learned, we derive our power bases from a number of sources. Often, our power bases may be driven by our values. No matter what the situation, our values will influence our behavior, either by helping to resolve differences or by ignoring them. How we adjust to a situation and the way in which we handle the circumstances (e.g., whether you like working alone or with a group) will ultimately be influenced by our values.

Now, let's look at who you are and what you value most in an organization.

INSIGHTS
INTO SELF

Directions: In order of importance, identify the three qualities you value the most. Then identify the three qualities you value the least.

Value   Value
Most   Least

____   ____   **Achievement**—making a worthwhile contribution to the organization for which I work

____   ____   **Beauty**—working in an attractive facility that provides pleasant working conditions

____   ____   **Caring**—working with people who consider me important, who are genuinely concerned about my welfare, and who are interested in how I feel about various situations

____   ____   **Egalitarianism**—working for an organization that provides equal opportunity for all employees, and in an environment conducive to expressing differing viewpoints when they occur

____   ____   **Excitement**—working for an organization that offers stimulating work for me and other individuals, where I have opportunities for professional growth

____   ____   **Freedom**—working for an organization where I can make choices, express my views and exert my independence

____   ____   **Fulfillment**—working for an organization that I feel has a meaningful mission

____   ____   **Integration**—working for an organization that possesses unity and wholeness, encourages expression of ideas, and is committed to its employees and to society

____   ____   **Structure**—being managed by a clear set of policies

Value Most	Value Least	
_____	_____	**Supportiveness**—working for an organization that supplies the necessary resources, tools and equipment required to accomplish my job
_____	_____	**Security**—feeling secure that my job is not in jeopardy—especially when my opinion differs from someone else's
_____	_____	**Successfulness**—working for an organization that is a leader in its field
_____	_____	**Warmth**—working for an organization that encourages friendly, open and informal relations among its employees

Values are an established set of guidelines that each of us has developed through the decision-making process. Values help establish consistent behavior patterns. Identifying your top three values reveals what is most important to you and the sources for differences you may find with others in the workplace.

SUMMARY

No single style determines whether you are maximizing your source of power or decision-making processes related to differences. What is important is that an individual who tries to influence a group uses the appropriate power base to define his or her leadership style and to persuade others legitimately to understand any differences in views.

In today's ever-changing and evolutionary approach to management, many organizations have moved away from reliance on power bases that emphasize compliance. These organizations have moved toward the use and integration of power bases, which will exert influence over others. Their intention is to enable individuals to speak up, without fear of expressing their differences. To best understand these concepts, in Section Three we will explore the various aspects of difference in the workplace and in social situations.

SECTION THREE

EXPLORING DIFFERENCES

Differences arise from behavioral assumptions drawn from attitudes. The various sources of differences (i.e., facts and information, methods, goals and values) illustrate the levels of difficulty you will encounter when resolving differences and disagreements. This section offers alternative strategies for responding to differences.

Conflicts may arise when differences are not acknowledged, dealt with and resolved. Differences are viewed as negative factors when the behaviors associated with some kind of difference are analyzed, based on assumptions about another person's attitudes.

Let's explore the behavioral pattern that people exhibit when differences arise.

Personal traits and characteristics are developed early on in life. As we grow and mature, we develop conditioned responses or habit patterns to numerous stimuli. We take many of our actions for granted, so that they almost become mechanical. The sum total of patterns is perceived by others as personality.

Some behaviors are easily adjusted, while others seem almost impossible to change. Often, the type of difference or one's maturity level determines how easy it is to make an adjustment.

The following four examples of differences are listed in the order of difficulty to resolve, from least difficult (i.e., facts and information) to most difficult (i.e., those issues which surround our systems of values and beliefs).

FOUR SOURCES
OF DIFFERENCES

1. Facts and Information

When differences of information or facts are at issue, two parties can see the same facts differently or can disagree on what the facts are. This is the easiest level to manage, because it can usually be resolved by sharing information and/or producing more reliable data.

2. Methods

This level presumes there is an agreed-upon common goal. Disagreements are about which strategies will be used to reach the goal(s) or about how to approach accomplishing something. Differences concerning methods assume that there is a common goal, so the differences can usually be resolved by defining a mutually acceptable strategy to reach the goal. While methods differences are fairly easy to manage, they are more difficult to resolve than differences concerning facts and information.

3. Goals

Here, differences occur with regard to achieving specific outcomes in basic goals. Disagreements often center on what should be done, what the focus is, what the common direction is, or whether there is a shared purpose. Collaboration (working together to come to an agreement on goals), negotiation and resolution skills can help to resolve the differences. Because all of the above elements are required to resolve differences, this level is more difficult to manage than the previous two.

4. Values

This is usually the most difficult level of difference to resolve. While the other levels usually deal with tangibles, value differences deal with ideology, basic principles and beliefs. People identify strongly with their values and can be very resistant to changing them. The issue becomes whether it is possible to work out a satisfactory outcome without one or the other party compromising their values. This requires a sensitive understanding and respect for each person's values, plus hard work to reach a win-win solution.

Differences may be difficult to resolve because each party may approach the issues from any one of the four levels. Also, as differences develop, they may start at one level and shift to a different one. A dialogue that begins with a statement of difference will never move on to the issues of agreement. To stabilize the levels, the parties must establish issues of agreement before they state issues of disagreement.

The graphic below correlates the four sources of conflict with the level of difficulty needed to resolve each one.

The Four Sources of Differences

Facts	*Methods*	*Goals*	*Values*

Easy to resolve   **Difficult to resolve**

Notice that facts and values are extreme opposites as sources of difference. Differences that move farther from informational disputes and closer to disputes over perception or value become increasingly difficult to resolve.

CHECK
UP

1. Which situation would be most difficult for you to resolve?

_____

_____

_____

_____

_____

_____

_____

_____

2. Reviewing the complexity of the difference, which level would be the easiest for you to deal with?

_____

_____

_____

_____

_____

_____

_____

_____

SOURCES OF DIFFERENCE

Now let's look at some scenarios and identify the source of the difference for each one.

Scenario #1

John and his coworker, Amanda, have been meeting for several weeks to develop departmental guidelines. During the course of the project, many differences have become apparent and John has become very uncomfortable working with Amanda.

Two weeks ago, when Amanda rejected his ideas, John felt Amanda wasn't taking his ideas seriously. Apart from the fact that his ideas were dismissed, his feelings were hurt. As a result, John canceled the last few meetings.

John wants to work as equals to accomplish this project on time and to resolve his differences with Amanda. He wants to incorporate both of their ideas. He decides to confront Amanda about his concerns and their differences of opinion.

QUESTION: What difference is at the source of this situation?

TASK: How would you respond in this situation? List things that would prevent this situation from escalating into an unpleasant and untenable work situation. Write down what you would say and do to resolve the differences.

Scenario #2

Janet and her coworker, Becky, have been asked to develop some department guidelines. The guidelines should have been completed by Friday, but they missed the deadline. Janet thinks they missed the deadline because Becky canceled the last two meetings. Janet doesn't understand why the meetings were canceled and is upset with Becky for canceling them. Janet feels that Becky is ignoring her.

In addition, Janet is very knowledgeable on the guidelines, but her boss asked her to collaborate on this project with Becky. Janet decides to approach Becky about the canceled meetings and the missed deadline.

QUESTION: What type of difference is at the source of the situation? What strategies do you think would get to the root of the problem?

TASK: Identify your ideal response in this situation. How would you go about learning the things you could do to resolve your differences? Write down what you would say to your coworker.

Scenario #3

Walter wants to take two days off from his job for a religious holiday. Walter's holiday is not recognized as a national or federal holiday. He asks his supervisor for the time off, explaining that it is for religious reasons; she refuses, stating, "We can't spare you at this time. There is too much work to be done."

Walter offers to work on the weekend or during one of the other holidays. His supervisor refuses, stating that one thing has nothing to do with the other.

As a result Walter feels hurt, angry and discriminated against for the lack of respect demonstrated toward his culture and religion.

QUESTION: What is the source of this difference? What issue(s) contribute to the difference?

TASK: How would you respond? How would you resolve the differences? How many obstacles would you need to overcome before you could resolve the situation? What actions would you take?

Hopefully, from working through these scenarios, you have gained some insight into your own behaviors, as well as to those of the other parties involved. As the scenarios demonstrate, differences can evolve into points of disagreement—you may be aware of some points while you may not recognize others. A disagreement continues when differences are not resolved. Your behavior patterns can affect another individual's ability to recognize and work toward resolving the issues stemming from your differences.

RESPONSES TO DIFFERENCES

As a child, you developed your own personal strategies for dealing with differences. Even if your strategies did not resolve differences successfully, you continued to use them because you were unaware of other alternatives. As an adult, you may act in much the same way.

Let's consider some alternatives to your old strategies. First, we will explore how these alternatives are part of a continuum of responses.

Difference-resolution strategies are classified into three categories:

- Avoidance

- Diffusion

- Confrontation

A Continuum of Responses to Difference Situations

		Power	Negotiation
Avoidance		*Diffusion*	*Confrontation*

Use this diagram as a springboard as you analyze the three categories of difference resolution. While we have discussed various ways to understand differences, there is a plethora of ways in which you can respond to a given situation or problem.

You will want to refer back to this avoidance-diffusion-confrontation continuum as you visualize the different behavioral manifestations described below, which occur when differences arise.

Avoidance

Some people attempt to avoid differences or difficult situations altogether. Such people tend to repress emotional reactions, ignore confrontation or detach from the situation entirely (e.g., quit a job, drop out of school, get a divorce). These individuals are either unable to confront their antagonists directly or they lack the skills to negotiate effectively.

Although avoidance may cover up differences, it does not leave the individual satisfied. Avoiding resolving differences is detrimental to an individual's ability to develop negotiation skills and the self-confidence required to resolve difficult situations.

Diffusion

Essentially delaying actions, diffusion strategies temper situations—at least temporarily. Focusing on minor points, while delaying discussion of the major problem or avoiding clarification of salient issues are examples of avoidance escalated to diffusion. Diffusion can be used to "muddy the waters," which renders confrontation impossible. As with avoidance strategies, diffusion leaves a person dissatisfied, anxious about the future and lacking in self-confidence.

Confrontation

The third major strategy involves directly confronting others to resolve differences. Confrontation is subdivided into power and negotiation strategies. Power strategies include physical force (e.g., violence), bribery (e.g., money, favors) and punishment (e.g., withholding love, money or promotion). These tactics are only effective if you have the upper hand in the situation.

The strategy to resolving differences helps to understand the need to find effective alternatives to old strategies, and to deal with differences in a way that does not involve the drawbacks discussed previously.

BEHAVIORAL MANIFESTATIONS
THAT ARISE FROM DIFFERENCES

We resort to various behavioral patterns when confronted with strong differences. Let's explore each pattern to get a better understanding of why we sometimes act the way we do when a conflict arises.

Rationalization: Rationalizations are excuses for an individual's inability to accomplish a specific goal.

Regression: An individual who has not reached his or her fullest level of maturity is unable to integrate various forms of coping mechanisms into his or her life. In such cases, this may result in the individual shutting down emotionally, withdrawing from a situation completely, or resorting to some sort of regressive behavioral pattern learned in childhood.

Fixation: In this form of behavior, the individual emotionally exhibits a repeated behavioral pattern. Each time that person experiences turmoil and differences, he or she acts out the same forms of behavior and expects a different result. Individuals with fixations must learn different methods with which they can deal with situations of difference.

Resignation: Apathy occurs after a period of prolonged frustration. People who have reached this point have typically lost all hope of accomplishing their goals, and have withdrawn from the situation completely. This is characteristic of people who find themselves in boring and mundane jobs, with little or no reward satisfaction, where there is virtually no hope for improvement or promotion.

Each of these behavioral patterns plays a major role in the way in which each person handles his or herself when faced with a difference of opinion. Various patterns of behavior will emerge, depending upon how vested and emotionally involved that person has become in the situation and what level the difference has reached.

As you read the following scenarios, notice how behavior can influence attitudes when differences of opinion are involved.

Scenario #1

This manager is concerned about employee relations. Although she feels this way, she doesn't necessarily want to get involved in a situation involving a disgruntled employee. Her concern is overshadowed by her need to avoid direct confrontation, therefore, she withdraws completely from the situation.

Scenario #2

This manager is also concerned about employee relations, but only to quiet what he perceives to be "the masses." He tells his workers what they can and can't do, without paving the way for any kind of open, give-and-take discussion.

Scenario #3

This manager is also concerned about employee relations. He approaches his employees and says, "Gee, I'm sorry. Do you want to air your feelings?" Unfortunately, when they express their feelings and concerns, he takes no action. In other words, no productivity was achieved through his behavior.

Scenario #4

This manager is concerned about employee relations. She approaches her workers and says: "I've heard about your problems, and I'm sorry. I'd like to give you the opportunity to air your grievances and concerns, so we can discuss the situation to move toward a more positive and productive working environment."

In this scenario, the manager can integrate tasks, relationships and workers.

As you can see from the four scenarios, similar values evoke drastically different behavior. Similarly, there are various ways to handle these differences. When dealing with differences, think about the results and the impact your decisions will have upon the other people involved. Be sure you are looking at the end result with a *qualitative* form of reasoning, rather than quantitative. Effective workers adapt their behavior to meet the needs of their colleagues, subordinates and their organization.

Your organization, for example, might achieve its highest productivity at the end of a quarter. But what profit is really to be made if workers are unhappy, resign and go to work for your competitor?

SUMMARY

The continuum of responses to various situations offers three options through which to deal with differences: avoidance, diffusion and confrontation. Behavioral patterns prior to a conflict are crucial to understanding the role you play in resolving existing differences. By being aware of your own behavior in difficult situations, you will be better able to resolve differences and disagreements.

SECTION FOUR

UNPACKING DIFFERENCES
Preconflict Strategies

We have seen that conflicts generally occur when issues remain unresolved and the differences between the parties are not properly addressed. Conflict allows us to learn, progress and grow. While there is no perfect paradigm for handling conflict, the basic strategy for reducing conflict is to find goals upon which the groups can agree and to reestablish valid communication among everyone involved. The objective of this strategy is a resolution that is beneficial for all parties. While conflict can result in a satisfactory resolution, most people find conflict undesirable and difficult to manage.

We recognize conflict when differences cause us to view the other party as the opposition or the enemy and when our perceptions of reality become distorted. When this happens, both parties will tend to focus on their own individual strengths. In addition, each will highlight the fallibilities and weaknesses of the "adversary." As hostility continues to increase, communication ceases. Lack of communication makes it easier to stay in a negative mode. Not communicating also makes it increasingly difficult to break down the barriers of false perceptions and work toward resolving existing differences.

If an intervention occurs at this point, with a mediator overseeing the differences (acting as a facilitator), the mediator is likely to find that the parties are not listening to one another. Instead, they are listening only for words that support their individual arguments. Their task is how to find a way to "unpack" their differences, a process that uses effective communication tools actively to resolve differences and disagreements.

The following paradigm can help explain how to unpack differences before they become a conflict.

PARADIGM OF PRECONFLICT

Four elements contribute to unpacking differences that create conflict.

1. Frustration

Frustration occurs when a person feels blocked from satisfying a goal-directed activity or concern. The concern may be clear or only vaguely defined; it may be of critical importance or only incidental to the ultimate goal. But the person feels distinctly that someone is getting in the way of his or her being able to attain an objective.

2. Conceptualization

Conceptualization involves asking key questions (i.e., What's going on here? Is this good or bad? What's the problem? and What issues are at stake?). While some conceptualizations may be almost instantaneous, others may develop after considerable thought. Conceptualizations may be very sharp and clear, or they may be fuzzy. Regardless of its inception, conceptualization forms the basis of the individual's reaction to frustration and how he or she will ultimately respond to differences.

3. Behaviors

Your behaviors flow out of conceptualizing and strategizing. Behaviors set in motion a pattern of interaction between the parties in conflict. In the course of this interaction, how each party conceptualizes the conflict may result in deepening frustration. The longer the pattern continues, the more entrenched the adversaries become in their own agendas and the more divergent differences become. As a result, new frustrations, hostility and resistance can develop from such situations.

4. Outcome

Outcome is the state of affairs that exists when differences are resolved. Outcomes may be either positive or negative (e.g., the decisions or actions taken and the feelings involved). If the outcome is negative it is most likely the result of residual frustration.

Residual frustration can generate new differences and plant the seeds for future conflicts. When this situation occurs, the individual may find him or herself in the situation where it is said that "the cure is worse than the disease."

Perhaps the most tragic illustration of this principle is seen by reviewing the lack of judgment shown by the diplomats who negotiated the Versailles Treaty following World War I. When the German generals surrendered to the Allied forces, they expected the peace treaty to be negotiated based on President Woodrow Wilson's respected "Fourteen Points" document.

Unfortunately, Wilson was terminally ill and unable to guide the peace process. British and French statesmen, embittered by the devastating fighting, wanted to punish Germany and forced the citizens to pay heavy war reparations for damages as part of the treaty.

Believing that they had been betrayed, the German people found it easy to listen to the propaganda and doctrine of hatred spread by the Nazi party. So great was their anger toward the French that the Nazi leaders initiated World War II and again attacked France. To make the source of the German nation's frustration clear, French leaders were forced to sign terms of unconditional surrender in the very same railroad car where, barely 20 years before, Germany had signed the Armistice.

CRITERIA FOR RESOLVING DIFFERENCES

You will find it helpful to assess the outcome of a preconflict resolution of differences using the following three criteria:

1. Was the quality of the decision or action that resulted creative, realistic and/or practical?

2. What was the psychological and physical condition of the differing parties upon resolution of the dispute?

3. What was the quality of the relationship between the differing parties? Was there mutual respect and understanding and were they willing to work together? Or was there hostility and intent to hurt?

These criteria also need to be reconsidered when determining how to behave when differences are not resolved and a conflict results. The criteria also apply to your evaluation of the cost and benefits that may have accrued. Obviously, the way the parties define the problem will greatly influence the chances for a constructive outcome and the feelings that will be mobilized during the confrontation.

THE PROS AND CONS OF CONFLICT

Although conflict may inflict destruction and unnecessary costs on individuals and organizations, conflict may also result in the attainment of goals, which enables adversaries ultimately to resolve their differences. Conflict is an engine of evolution that allows you to learn, progress and grow.

Consider the following assumptions:

1. Conflict is an inevitable and important human process.

2. Conflicts are likely to increase in times of change.

3. Conflicts can have either creative or destructive results.

4. Those who understand the processes and dynamics of conflict are better able to deal with the situation, increasing individuals' chances for creative outcomes while minimizing destructive results.

As we've stated, there is no perfect paradigm for handling conflict. The basic strategy for resolving differences in a preconflict stage is to find goals upon which the parties can agree; then reestablish valid communication with everyone involved. Pursuing this strategy will help resolve difficult situations and what may initially appear to be unresolvable differences. Taking the initiative and being proactive can resolve or, at the very least, reduce differences before they escalate into conflicts.

RESPONSES TO CONFLICTS

In a utopian organization, differences would never turn into conflicts. Since, however, we do not live or work in an edenistic society, the most realistic goal is to minimize our differences and best resolve the conflict before long-term damage has been done.

A manager should emphasize the contributions and interaction between groups and not just the end result (i.e., the goal). This involves developing a reward system and, whenever possible, providing employees with new projects to broaden those employees' growth opportunities. Also, a manager should establish a basis for fostering understanding and goodwill among employees.

ELEMENTS OF CONFLICT

Conflict is comprised of three components:

> *Expressed struggle*—either verbal or nonverbal
>
> *Interdependence*—symbiosis
>
> *Perceived interference*—incompatible goals

POSITIVE AND NEGATIVE
ASPECTS OF CONFLICT

Directions: Read the questions below and think back to situations you have encountered. Doing so will enable you to look at your personal reaction to positive and negative conflict.

1. What are some positive results from conflict at:

   a) Work—both to the individual and the organization?

   _____

   _____

   b) Home—both to the spouse and to the family (i.e., children and relatives)?

   _____

   _____

2. What are some negative outcomes from conflict at:

   a) Work—both to the individual and the organization?

   _____

   _____

   b) Home—both to the spouse and to the family (i.e., children and relatives)?

   _____

   _____

   What were your responses? _____

   Did you find a common thread? _____

   Do you have some preventive measures in mind?

   _____

GOALS AND CONFLICT

Goals should be high enough that the individual is consistently challenged to meet them, but realistic enough that they can be attained. Consider the elements of the following situation, where the established goal caused a conflict.

A managing editor assigned an assistant editor a two-day deadline to review a lengthy manuscript. The assistant editor could not begin work until the managing editor and stakeholders finished reviewing the manuscript.

The assistant editor didn't receive the managing editor's and stakeholders' comments until a half-day before the deadline. Because of the time crunch, the assistant editor went to the managing editor and requested an extension of his deadline. His request was refused.

Given the time constraints, it was impossible for the assistant editor to meet his deadline. He felt angry, unwilling and unmotivated to continue working on the manuscript and resigned from his position. The project was left uncompleted.

Ideally, the managing editor would have managed their differences by realizing that the original goal for the assistant editor was no longer feasible. He would have said, "I realize your timelines were cut, so you're unable to complete the project. If, however, you can do whatever is feasible by close of business today, I will certainly note your efforts and explain the situation to the editor-in-chief."

In spite of the difficulty, this simple gesture of understanding and goodwill probably would have motivated the assistant editor to complete the task. Positive reinforcement, rather than punishment, would have helped the employee to achieve the senior editor's goal.

NEGATIVE AND POSITIVE
OUTCOMES OF CONFLICT

The following are negative outcomes of conflict:

- Debilitation
- Distraction from achieving your goals
- Defensiveness and rigidity
- Distortion of reality
- Negative cycles
- Escalation and proliferation of additional conflicting issues

These are positive outcomes of conflict:

- Increased motivation and energy
- Clarification of issues and positions
- Building of self and group awareness
- Results that lead to innovation and creativity
- Outlet for resolving internal conflicts
- Creation of better interpersonal relationships

STAGES OF CONFLICT

Due to a misunderstanding and/or lack of communication at the outset, differences among partners frequently result in conflict. If and when a conflict arises, it's important to know that there are three stages of conflict. As you will see, some stages can yield positive results, while others may prove detrimental to all parties.

"*I win–you lose*" occurs when conflict is inevitable and agreement becomes impossible. In simplistic terms, this comes down to the "somebody's going to win, somebody's going to lose" power struggle. In this situation, when an individual believes agreement is impossible, behavior will range from passive to active. If the stakes are low, the individual may be passive enough to let fate decide the outcome of the conflict.

When the stakes are moderate, a third party may be called upon to decide the outcome of the conflict. When, however, the stakes are riding high, the situation deteriorates. At this point, individuals will actively engage in an "I win–you lose" power struggle, which results in only one perceived winner.

"*Lose–lose*" presents itself when a conflict may not be prevented—when stakes are high and both parties are emotionally involved. In this instance, people will eventually isolate themselves from the situation at hand, with both parties ultimately withdrawing into their own corners.

"*Win–win*" conflicts can be detected early on in a conflict. This situation makes it possible for intervention to occur. In addition, in "win–win" situations the stakes are lowered to permit mediation by a neutral third party. This kind of mediation can aid in the belief that agreement is possible even though a conflict exists. Because of the behavior that occurs in this stage of conflict, "win–win" situations are known for being action-oriented, enabling an individual to move toward an active problem-solving mode.

As you can see, very real, negative consequences may result from mismanagement and misunderstanding. Such situations can be debilitating and can distract from achieving your goals. Conflict can contribute to the increased defensiveness and rigidity of everyone involved—it can distort reality, contribute to a negatively reinforcing cycle, escalate or make the situation more egregious and generate additional issues that will require resolution.

If you can accurately assess the attitudes an individual or group possesses about a potential conflict and gauge what the stakes are, you can most often predict the other person's or the group's behavior (and vice-versa).

SUMMARY

Conflicts can occur when differences are not properly managed or resolved. When this happens, the parties view one another as the enemy. As hostility between individuals increases, communication ceases to function and differences can become completely unresolvable. Thus, you must learn to "unpack" or to assess the situation.

In the unpacking process, you effectively use communication tools to resolve differences and disagreements. The way the parties define the problem greatly influences the chances for a constructive outcome.

By assessing the attitudes an individual or group possesses about a potential conflict, and gauging what the stakes are, we can usually predict the other person's or the group's behavior, thus preventing (or offsetting) the magnitude and scope of the conflict. Using these techniques can help prevent differences from escalating to a state of conflict.

SECTION FIVE

MANAGING DIFFERENCES

Most people view differences in a negative light—as something bad that must be avoided, minimized, or eliminated. Differences can also be viewed positively—as opportunities for learning and growth and for developing new social skills that can help a person communicate more effectively with others. Like other skills, learning to resolve one's differences is something that can be taught. And, if managed constructively, differences can become sources of innovation and energy.

Left unmanaged, differences can drain creativity and energy. Managing differences effectively will help minimize a potentially negative outcome and maximize the opportunities to attain desired goals.

The goal is to learn skillfully to manage and resolve personal and professional differences, while furthering the potentially constructive outcomes. We must learn to develop ways in which our skills for resolution of differences can be assimilated and used—both cerebrally and intuitively.

IDENTIFYING STYLES OF MANAGING DIFFERENCES

Identifying the various sources of differences is the first step in learning how effectively to manage disagreements and ultimately to work toward a resolution. The second step is to identify how we have typically managed differences, which is an individual's "preferred style."

At an early age, each of us learned how to survive and take care of ourself. Whether we knew it or not, we learned about resolving differences from a variety of sources:

Childhood messages (e.g., "Why is a pretty girl like you interested in science? Most girls wouldn't even want to compete in the science fair.")

Watching others (e.g., the way your parents, friends, coworkers, and mentors manage their differences) If you were employed in a business where a tyrannical boss frequently and publicly "called people on the carpet," you never learned how to deal with or resolve differences of opinion in the workplace.

Past experience (e.g., the way we have handled differences in the past influences the way in which we respond to differences now) If you have never had to work out a compromise solution, you may see differences from a strictly black-and-white point of view (i.e., "It's either my way or nothing.").

Predominant style (e.g., regardless of how you learned to handle differences, you have a predominant way of dealing with a difficult situation.) If you are someone who is inclined to sacrifice your views to appease others, you may not know how properly to express your feelings or communicate your differences to others, and you would not be able to work toward a mutually beneficial resolution.

DETERMINING YOUR STYLE OF HANDLING DIFFERENCES

Most likely, you learned your preferred method of handling differences during your childhood. Your inherently unique style has been influenced by your upbringing, your experiences and the world around you.

The following questionnaire is designed to give you information about your preferred method of dealing with differences. It will help you to identify the style you presently use to resolve your differences. Once you know your style, you can analyze your preferred method and assess its value to you.

The style that you'll determine from the questionnaire only indicates your *preferred* style. No style is set in stone. While you might have a predominant preferred style in various situations (e.g., in personal relationships), your style will change in other situations (e.g., in high-pressured, work-related situations).

YOUR STYLE
OF MANAGING
DIFFERENCES

Directions: Following are pairs of statements that describe possible responses to a situation of difference. As you read each statement, imagine yourself in a work, school or home environment, and visualize situations in which your wishes are different from someone else's. For each pair, circle the "A" or "B" statement that most closely typifies how you would respond.

1. A. There are times when I let others take responsibility for solving the problem.

   B. Rather than negotiate an agreement, I try to resolve only what the other person and I agree upon.

2. A. I tend to find a compromise for both parties during a difference of opinion.

   B. I try to soothe the other person's feelings to preserve our relationship.

3. A. I usually remain firm in the pursuit of my goals.

   B. I might try to soothe the other person's feelings to preserve our relationship.

4. A. I try to find a compromise when there are differing points of view.

   B. I sometimes sacrifice my own point of view for that of another person.

5. A. I consistently seek another person's help in resolving differences.

   B. I usually try to resolve differences on my own.

6. A. I am willing to do what is necessary to avoid tension when there is a difference between myself and another person.

   B. I try to win my position.

7. A. I try to postpone dealing with differences until I've had time to think over the situation.

    B. I will concede some of my points in exchange for others.

8. A. I do not often change my goals.

    B. I attempt to get all concerns and issues immediately out in the open.

9. A. Differences are not always worth worrying about.

    B. I make some effort to get my way in spite of differences.

10. A. I'm firm in pursuing my goals.

    B. I try to find a compromise solution.

11. A. I attempt to get all differences out in the open as soon as possible.

    B. I might try to soothe the other person's feelings to preserve our relationship.

12. A. I sometimes avoid taking a position that would create controversial differences.

    B. I'll concede certain issues to the other person if he or she will concede some to me.

13. A. I will propose finding a middle ground.

    B. I press issues of difference to make my points.

14. A. I tell the other person my ideas and ask for his or hers in return.

    B. I try to persuade the other party to accept the merits of my position.

15. A. I might try to soothe the other person's feelings to preserve our relationship, in spite of the differences.

    B. I try to do what is necessary to avoid tension when there are differences.

16. A. I try not to hurt the other person's feelings if we have differences.

    B. I try to convince the other person to accept the merits of my position.

17. A. I'm usually firm in pursuing my goals.

    B. I try to convince the other person to accept the merits of my position.

18. A. If it makes the other party happy, I might let a group maintain their point of view.

    B. I'll concede certain issues to the other person if he or she will concede some to me.

19. A. I try to get all concerns and issues immediately out in the open.

    B. I try to postpone the issue until I've had time to think it over.

20. A. I immediately attempt to work through the differences people have between them.

    B. I try to find a fair balance of gains and losses for both people.

21. A. In approaching negotiations, I try to be considerate of the other person's wishes.

    B. I always lean toward a direct discussion of the problem.

22. A. I try to find a position intermediate between the other person's position and my own.

    B. I try to convince the other person of the merits of my position.

23. A. I'm often concerned with satisfying everyone's wishes.

    B. At times, I let others take responsibility for solving the problem.

24. A. If another person's position seems very important to them, I try to meet their wishes.

    B. I try to get the other person to compromise his or her position.

25. A. I try to show the other person the advantages of my position.

    B. In approaching negotiations, I try to be considerate of the other person's wishes.

26. A. I propose a middle ground to resolve differences.

    B. I'm nearly always concerned with satisfying the wishes of all parties.

27. A. I sometimes avoid taking positions that would create controversy.

    B. If it makes the other person happy, I might concede my differences and accept their position.

28. A. I usually pursue my goals firmly.

    B. I usually seek the other person's help in working out a solution to our differences.

29. A. I propose a middle ground to resolve differences.

    B. I feel that differences are not always worth worrying about.

30. A. I try not to hurt the other person's feelings.

    B. I communicate the problem to the person so we can work out our differences.

Scoring Key

For each of your responses on the questionnaire, circle the appropriate letter on the following chart. Then count the total number of circled letters in each column and record that number on the TOTALS line. The highest total is your preferred style.

	COMPETING FORCING	COLLABORATING PROBLEM-SOLVING	COMPROMISING SHARING	AVOIDING WITHDRAWAL	ACCOMMODATING SMOOTHING
1.				A	B
2.		B	A		
3.	A				B
4.			A		B
5.		A		B	
6.	B			A	
7.			B	A	
8.	A	B			
9.	B			A	
10.	A		B		
11.		A			B
12.			B	A	
13.	B		A		
14.	B	A			
15.				B	A
16.	B				A
17.	A			B	
18.			B		A
19.		A		B	
20.		A	B		
21.		B		A	
22.	B		A		
23.		A		B	
24.			B		A
25.	A				B
26.		B	A		
27.				A	B
28.	A	B			
29.			A	B	
30.		B			A
TOTALS					

67

Scoring

When it comes to behaviors that manage differences, there are no right or wrong answers. All five styles are useful in certain situations; each represents a distinct set of useful social skills.

Conventional wisdom, for example, recognizes that often "two heads are better than one" (collaboration). At the same time it says to "kill your enemies with kindness" (accommodation), "split the difference" (compromise), "leave well enough alone" (avoidance) and "might makes right" (competition). The effectiveness of a style for managing differences depends upon the requirements of the given situation and the skill with which that management style is used.

We are all capable of using all five difference-management styles; there is no one characteristic or ideal style when it comes to dealing with difficult situations. Some individuals use certain styles better than others, and other people rely upon one style more heavily than others—for whatever reason (e.g., temperament or practice).

The different management behaviors you use are, therefore, a result of both your personal predispositions and the requirements of the situation at hand.

With this in mind, you can interpret your scores.

Interpreting Your Scores

Note: Each possible score is graphed in relation to other people who have completed the instrument in the past.

It's important that we learn how to work through our patterns, so that we can use the style most appropriate for a situation. Consider the following:

How surprised are you about your preferred style?

_____

_____

What did you learn about your preferred style for handling differences?

_____

_____

What are the strengths of your style?

_____

_____

What are the drawbacks of your preferred style?

_____

_____

How does your score differ from your prediction?

_____

_____

What strengths of your style can help you deal effectively with differences in your personal relationships?

_____

_____

What areas of your style require improvement for you effectively to manage differences in your personal relationships?

_____

_____

How does the chart match your job role?

_____

_____

What risks are involved with using your style at your job?

_____

_____

What are your strengths in dealing with the differences between others at your workplace?

_____

_____

What areas can you improve upon in dealing with differences in your workplace?

_____

_____

FIVE STYLES FOR MANAGING DIFFERENCES

You've just explored the process of managing differences by using the appropriate style for the situation. Now, we will discuss how people use their preferred styles.

Five styles are appropriate for managing differences: competition, accommodation, avoidance, collaboration and compromise. All of the styles have their strengths. Understanding your style is the key to handling a given situation.

Competition is a power-oriented, win-lose approach. You use whatever power you have available to win, forcing the other party to concede his or her differences.

Accommodation is the opposite of competition. When accommodating, you neglect your own differences and yield to those of the other person.

Avoidance is side-stepping or, at least, postponing the airing of any differences. By avoidance, consciously or subconsciously you choose not to resolve any differences. In this way, you avoid a confrontation.

Compromise is splitting the difference, giving a little and taking a little, seeking a middle ground. Compromise falls somewhere in between competition and collaboration. Both parties get some, but not all, of what they want.

Collaboration is win-win, aimed at finding the best possible solution, using all available ideas and resources that fully satisfy the needs of both parties. Both parties to try to identify underlying concerns and differences and to find alternatives that meet everyone's needs.

Things to keep in mind as you work through differences:

- There are almost always differences in viewpoint between two or more individuals or parties over a given issue at any point in time.

- Differences become apparent when multiple parties are concerned about turf, resources, rewards, functions and technical issues.

- Differences are inevitable.

- Differing viewpoints are useful and necessary for creativity.

Differences can lead to either competition or collaboration. The reward structure that is in place in any social situation provides the incentive for the differences to result in a productive or destructive situation. If only limited reward is available, one person is forced to win and the other must lose; the situation will be competitive. On the other hand, if it is possible for all parties involved to achieve their goals, and the achievement of one person's goals involves or leads to goal achievement by another, the situation is collaborative.

It's not hard to think of examples of pure competitive and collaborative situations. A serious tennis game or the interaction between a prospective car buyer and a used car dealer are purely competitive situations. An army squad in combat or several people working on a joint research project are collaborative situations.

The behaviors most appropriate and effective in a competitive situation are quite different from, and often directly opposite to, behaviors that are most effective in a collaborative situation. Following is a partial list of behaviors or strategies appropriate and effective in each type of situation:

EFFECTIVE COMPETITIVE BEHAVIOR

1. Behavior is directed toward achieving personal goals and resolving differences.

2. Secrecy—the parties make sure the opponents don't know the differences and goals they want to achieve.

3. While accurately understanding one's own needs and differences, the parties keep them either hidden or misrepresented. If others do not know exactly what an individual wants and how much he or she wants it, they don't know what that person is willing to give up to get it.

4. Unpredictable, mixed strategies use the element of surprise.

5. The parties use threats and bluffs to take each other by surprise.

6. Illogical or irrational arguments are used to defend a position to which the parties are strategically committed.

7. When teams, committees, or organizations are involved, each group communicates negative stereotypes of the other group, ignoring logic, and convincing others they mean business.

EFFECTIVE COLLABORATIVE BEHAVIOR

1. Behavior is directed toward resolving differences and, ultimately, achieving common goals.

2. Parties are open in discussing, settling and resolving differences.

3. The parties understand and accurately represent their needs and differences.

4. Predictability—although flexible behavior is appropriate, it is not designed to take the other party by surprise.

5. Threats and bluffs are not used to take the other person by surprise.

6. Parties use logical and innovative processes to defend their views and to settle differences—when they are convinced the viewpoints are valid—or try to find solutions to problems.

7. Success demands that stereotypes are dropped, that differences are openly discussed and that all ideas are given consideration on their merit. Good working relationships are maintained. Positive feelings about others are both a cause and an effect of collaboration.

Most of the social and professional situations in which we find ourselves are neither purely competitive nor purely collaborative. One complication is that, by default, we all must play the competitive and collaborative games simultaneously. This occurs most commonly when we try to problem-solve with the same persons with whom we are competing for promotion, or when work groups that are vying for the highest performance ratings must also work together to complete an assignment.

The cynic approaches every situation as if it were a competitive game, transforming every discussion into a debate. A naive individual may be in danger of approaching every situation as if it were a collaborative game. The realist may recognize the objective reality of the situation and choose dual approaches that are appropriate for the coexisting conditions.

The common problem in the workplace today is cynicism. We characteristically approach situations as if they were competitive games when, in fact, they are not. In the early decades of industrialization, worker-management relations were conducted in a strictly win-lose style, as if the entire process were competitive bargaining (i.e., what the workers gained, management lost, and vice versa). Attitudes do shift over time and parties now realize that a more collaborative approach to managing oneself and others achieves better results.

Attitudinal change is key to using collaborative behavior as a substitute for competitive behavior and to resolve differences. Parties need to begin to know each other and to regard one another with some measure of trust. Establishing trust allows us to achieve the harmony that leads to the mutual respect of each party's differences. Then, the parties can begin to examine the situation to find its collaborative aspects.

Now, let's continue to explore the different characteristics and facets of collaborative and competitive behaviors.

Collaborations

1. Win-win
2. Flexible
3. Make concessions in turn
4. Ask questions and explore positions
5. Usually interested in the other party's needs

Competition

1. Win-lose
2. Adversarial
3. Inflexible
4. No concessions
5. Don't ask questions or explore positions
6. Not interested in the other party's needs

CHECK
UP

1. Under what conditions would you use competitive behavior to resolve differences?

_____

_____

_____

_____

2. Under what conditions would you use collaborative behavior to resolve differences?

_____

_____

_____

_____

3. What factors cause you to misread a given situation and what are the differences that may arise on such occasions?

_____

_____

_____

_____

After exploring the various aspects of collaborative and competitive behavior, does it surprise you to learn that collaboration is the best strategy to use to manage differences? Unfortunately, in many situations, you may not have the opportunity to use purely collaborative behaviors to resolve differences. In those cases, you can still work toward a positive resolution of differences. Just recognize that competitive behaviors will affect your ability to achieve your goals.

CONFLICT
STYLE
ACTION PLAN

Now that you've learned about managing differences and some strategies that enable you to resolve differences collaboratively, you can begin to capitalize on what you've learned by completing the following Action Plan.

1. The three most important things I learned about managing differences are:

a. _____

b. _____

c. _____

2. In light of Item 1, I plan to take the following three actions more often:

a. _____

b. _____

c. _____

3. In light of Item 1, I plan to do the following less often:

a. _____

b. _____

c. _____

4. The three obstacles to accomplishing these changes are:

a. _____

b. _____

c. _____

5. I can overcome these three obstacles listed above by changing the following behavioral problems:

a. _____

b. _____

c. _____

6. I'll know I've successfully managed my differences effectively when:

a. _____

b. _____

7. Two people who can help me to manage differences in a more constructive manner are:

a. _____

b. _____

YOUR BEHAVIOR FOR RELATING TO DIFFERENCES IS SITUATIONAL

Directions: Write down the names or initials of three people with whom you work closely or who are significant to you. Then, record what style you primarily use for managing differences when interacting with each of these people.

Name/Initials   **Difference Management Style**

1. _____   _____

2. _____   _____

3. _____   _____

From your knowledge of collaborative and competitive climates, coupled with what you have learned from reading this book, you should have some clear ideas about your personal style for handling differences. Before you begin to apply your skills to difficult situations, you'll want to learn more about the intricacies of managing differences.

MANAGING REAL OR
VALUE DIFFERENCES

Managing differences requires a particular set of skills that must be learned and practiced. These skills include your:

- Ability to assess and diagnose the nature of the differences

- Effectiveness in initiating confrontations

- Ability to grasp the other person's point of view

- Use of the problem-solving process to bring about a consensus decision

Diagnosis

Diagnosing the nature of a difference is the starting point in any problem-solving process. The most important thing that you must determine is whether a difference is ideological (i.e., value) or real (i.e., tangible), or a combination of the two. Value differences are extremely difficult to resolve.

If, for example, my cultural background suggests that women should be treated as the equals of men in every phase of public and private life, and your culture stresses that women should be protected or even prohibited from certain areas, we have a difference in values that makes it difficult for us to find a point of agreement about behavior that would satisfy us both.

If the issue is a difference in values resulting in intangible effects on both parties, it is best tolerated. If, however, a tangible effect occurs, you will want to work especially hard to resolve the differences.

Initiation

Taking the initiative to confront your fellow worker, spouse or friend is both effective and essential to resolving differences. It's important not to begin by attacking or demeaning the opposing party. When confronting an issue, never assume a defensive posture. Such posturing is merely a stumbling block when it comes to resolving differences. The most effective way for you to confront the other party is to state the tangible effects the difference has on you.

For example: "I have a problem. Due to your stance on overnight travel, I'm unable to apply for the supervisory position that I feel I'm qualified to handle." This approach is more effective than your saying, "You're discriminating against me because of my child-care responsibilities—typical of all men." Confrontation is not synonymous with verbal attacks.

Listening

After you've initiated a confrontation, hear the other person's point of view. Defensive rebuttals often ensue when the initial statement made by one person is not what the other was hoping to hear. Avoid argument-provoking replies. Also, do not attempt to defend yourself, explain your position, or make demands or threats. Instead, engage in reflective or active listening by paraphrasing or clarifying the other person's position. Only after you've interpreted the opposition's view in a manner that is satisfactory to the other person should you reiterate your point of view—avoiding value statements.

Make sure you place the focus on tangible outcomes. Usually, when we listen to the opposition, our adversary's power lowers, along with his or her defenses; the opposition becomes more willing to hear our point of view. Of course, if both parties involved are skilled in active listening, the chances of resolving differences successfully is greatly enhanced.

Problem Solving

The final skill necessary to successfully resolve a difference is problem-solving. The steps in this process are simple and easy to apply.

1. Clarify the problem. What is the tangible difference? Where does each party stand on the issue?

2. Generate and evaluate a number of possible solutions. Often, these two actions should be taken exclusive of one another. First, raise all possible differences and then brainstorm for solutions to each difference. Then, evaluate each proposed solution.

3. Decide together (do not vote) on the best solution. The solution most acceptable to all parties should be chosen.

4. Plan the implementation of the solution. How will the solution be executed? When will it be executed?

5. Plan for an evaluation of the solution after a specific period of time. This step is essential. Why? Because the first solution chosen is not always the best or most workable in the end. If the first solution presents problems, repeat each of the five steps.

Together, these steps are effective strategies for managing real or value differences. If you want to achieve meaningful resolution of differences, these skills are basic requirements. In addition to these steps, be aware that various signals could lead to conflicts.

SIGNALS

The signals that indicate a difference between yourself and others are important. Many of these signals are visceral, while others are intuitive. Some signals may trigger feelings within you, with the velocity of a 7.1 on a Richter scale, and may result in your inability to manage the situation successfully.

Emotions play a powerful role in such instances. You may be the type of individual who takes great pains in hiding your anger, fear or depression. When emotions run high, a heated debate may follow. If you or another party loses control, coping with the key issues of difference can be extremely difficult, if not impossible.

When you know *when, what* or *who* sets you off, you'll be better able to recognize and confront not only your own anger and emotional outbursts, but also those of others.

Let's explore four elements that serve as a guiding light when dealing with managing differences.

DEALING WITH EMOTIONAL SITUATIONS

Four basic elements provide excellent guidance when the climate escalates to an emotional level.

1. Separate the people from the problem.
When people and problems meld, emotions have become entangled with the objective merits of the problem. Taking positions and refusing to let

go of your differences makes the situation worse, because egos become identified with the individuals involved. To resolve their differences, people must come to see themselves as working side by side, attacking the problem, not each other.

2. Focus on interests, not positions.

Your position can often obscure what it is you really want. Masking your true interests to maintain a certain position is not likely to produce an effective resolution of your differences or a lasting agreement for either party.

3. Invent options for mutual gain.

Free yourself from the constraints that prevent you from reaching optimal solutions. These may include conditions such as organizational pressure or the scrutiny of an adversary. Instead, set aside a designated timeframe within which you can discuss your differences. Create a wide range of possible solutions that will advance the group's shared interest, while you reconcile the disputed issues.

4. Insist on using objective criteria.

Determine some fair standard, independent of anyone's will. Avoid defensive positions and adamantly stating what you are willing or unwilling to do. It will then be possible to discuss objective criteria as well as your differences, so that you and the other party can achieve an equitable solution.

While these four elements provide skillful strategies in managing differences, they do not reveal one of the most vital ingredients in the resolution of differences—negotiation. With negotiation strategies, both sides can win.

The chief objective of negotiation is to resolve differences through compromise or to find a mutually satisfying solution for all parties involved. Negotiations provide the most positive and the least negative byproducts of all strategies aimed at managing differences.

NEGOTIATING TO WIN

Many managers view negotiation as an act that is legally executed over a bargaining table (e.g., a lawsuit). From this perspective, the term "negotiation" takes on a derogatory connotation. Applied appropriately, negotiation is a powerful and invaluable tool in mediating, managing, and resolving differences.

When selling your ideas to the opposing party, you can use negotiation to influence, convince and persuade.

PRINCIPLES OF PERSUASIVE NEGOTIATION

To develop negotiating skills, you must first accept the role of the negotiator. In simple terms, this means placing yourself in the mode enabling yourself to think and act like a negotiator.

Seven basic principles can be of great assistance to any negotiator. These principles are commonly known by the acronym, "TED'S PIG":

Trustworthiness—Does your opponent view you as credible? Are you trustworthy enough for your opposition to negotiate with you?

Expertise—This relates to informational power. Are you perceived as an expert, as an individual who possesses certain information that is of great value or is highly integral to the issue at hand? If so, you may hold the upper hand in the negotiation process.

Dynamism—Are you dynamic in your personal or professional life? Are you the type of person who's dynamic in *both* of these environments? People like being around a dynamic individual. Charisma can have a terrifically persuasive influence on the negotiation process.

Sympathy—Are you sympathetic toward the other person's point of view? Sympathy does not require you to go overboard in your feelings and actions so that you come out of a negotiation feeling you've been "taken for a ride." Sympathy does require your earnest attempt to understand the differences, views and positions held by the other individuals(s).

Power—As we discussed earlier, power is one of the most important elements to persuasion. Used effectively and in an appropriate manner, power can be the key to your entire negotiation.

Idealism—Are you the type of individual who seeks the best from a situation? Do you contribute your ideas in a manner that is perceived as positive to your organization? Both questions directly relate to idealism, which many people confuse with naivete. In negotiation situations, the two are in no way synony-mous. Masterful negotiators are anything but naive! When using the seven principles to persuasion, idealism can be extremely useful in defusing a situa-tion, or in mediating between all the parties involved in the dispute.

Goodwill—Is your outlook one of genuine concern for the welfare and well-being of others? Do you try to find the solution that is best for all the parties involved? Do you come across as wanting others to truly succeed in their endeavors?

This kind of genuineness lends itself to opening the discussion of dif-ferences. If the differences are aired properly, successful negotiation can yield workable, long term solutions.

Individuals possessed with goodwill are, in fact, truly interested in hearing the opposition's side. Each party learns about the other party's differ-ences, so that resolution will be genuinely beneficial to all participants.

These seven principles to persuasion are indeed food for thought. Their importance lies in how and if you use any one or all of them during a nego-tiation process. Each principle can be a powerful bargaining chip for you.

STRATEGIES FOR EFFECTIVE NEGOTIATION

Successful negotiation requires a combination of the principles of persuasion and effective behavior patterns. By assessing the situation, you will be able to gauge which of these principles would be the most beneficial to you as a negotiator. And it is equally important to develop a strategic plan for approach-ing your differences with a specific individual or group.

We'll use the negotiation process to buy a car as an example of the ten strategies that can be used to create a winning behavior plan:

1. Do your homework.

Always attempt to negotiate differences armed with knowledge. If you have to be *"armed"* at all, this is most likely the most positive contribution you can make. Noted author Steven Covey puts it plainly, "Seek first to understand, then to be understood." In addition to practical demographic information, this means doing your best to avoid stereotypes and to demon-strate that you are interested in exploring creative solutions.

2. Everything is negotiable.

Most negotiators start with an ideal or even an "in your dreams" objective. Smart negotiators recognize that this ideal is not their true goal. The goal is to find a solution acceptable to all parties involved. When purchasing a car, this means identifying a price that the buyer will pay, that the bank will authorize for a loan, that the sales manager will accept so that the salesperson can make their sales commission.

3. Never pay the sticker price.

Since everything is negotiable, the sticker price is only the car company's ideal price and its first bid. In some cases, the sticker price only indicates the maximum amount the car dealer can sell the car for and still remain competitive.

4. Bid low and haggle.

This is your opportunity to let the salesperson know your dream goal.

5. Don't commit yourself to anything.

Negotiation is only talking—the opportunity to explore options.

6. Start slowly and be patient.

If you are in too much of a hurry, you probably will not find a solution that satisfies all of the parties.

7. Crunch early and often.

Crunching is the judicious application of pressure, telling the other party you are not satisfied by their offer. For example, when the salesperson writes out a price proposal for the car that you think is too high, you may "crunch" by saying, "I think you need to sharpen your pencil better."

8. Make smaller concessions—especially toward the end.

As you get nearer to an acceptable offer, preserve your resources.

9. Keep looking for alternatives.

Creative solutions are seldom the first things we suggest—some solutions won't even occur to you until you begin to talk and brainstorm.

10. Leave your opponent feeling that they have done well.

Anyone who leaves a negotiation feeling negatively will be back, perhaps with a vengeance.

These are the bare essentials to managing differences. Take one step at a time. You are not going to become a successful negotiator overnight. It takes a lot of practice, patience and hands-on experience. Once you become comfortable with the basic art of negotiation, you will want to improve your ability to achieve a "win-win solution."

INTEREST VERSUS
POSITIONAL BARGAINING

A "win-win solution" is, of course, a natural extension of the "win-win" conflict; it gives true satisfaction to all parties affected by differences. Any negotiation team that achieves a win-win solution is to be congratulated. A negotiation team that creates a win-win solution when the differences point to another kind of conflict is an example to follow.

Experienced negotiators suggest that the ability to create a win-win solution when the odds are against you is the defining ability of a skilled negotiator. This ability is dependent largely on the negotiator's understanding of *interest* bargaining versus *positional* bargaining.

Positional bargainers act much like debaters: they present a case, demand change and evaluate their success based on their ability to achieve their aims. In a sense, their attitude is "let the best man win." A positional bargainer is lucky when he or she finds some middle ground for compromise. Once in a while, when resources are abundant, priorities do not conflict and value systems are similar, everybody gets everything they want. More often than not, someone goes home less than satisfied.

An interest bargainer looks at the differences between his or her own position and that of the other party, and tries to establish why the various positions are being held. The interest bargainer recognizes that a difference or a demand may, in fact, be largely symbolic and/or symptomatic of a larger issue.

For example, a well-known business organization established a conservative dress code that dictated that male employees must keep their hair cut above collar length and are not permitted to wear beards. However, some religious cultures in countries where they operate require adult men to wear full beards. The firm had the option to take a hard-line stance, but it looked beyond the differences and realized that, in such cases, wearing a beard is a cultural norm that generates respect. By recognizing the employees' rationale for their position, the firm adjusted the dress code for those men when they are doing business in their own country. And, if a man accepts a long-term assignment in the United States, he is required to conform to the dress code and is only permitted to wear a mustache.

In other situations, an employee who refuses to observe a company's dress code or other convention may be acting out a purely symbolic message. For instance, when a company known for its tradition of gathering employee feedback about policies and procedures issues a memorandum outlining a new dress code for its professional staff, one employee who was known for her aversion to conventional business dress continued to wear jeans to the office. She did so primarily because there had been no discussion or opportunity for employee input into the new policy. Management soon realized that its arbitrary decision was a mistake, and the woman was not reprimanded for her violation of the dress code. Instead, her direct supervisor requested that until a new policy was worked out, she follow the guidelines when interacting with customers or members of the corporate hierarchy.

A negotiator who develops the ability to resolve differences in a way that allows the parties concerned to obtain their interests rather than just their demands opens the door to far more creative solutions. Differences are more likely to be resolved faster and with less effort.

But what happens to the negotiator when the interest at the heart of the difference cannot be satisfied? Has the negotiator then backed him or herself into an even tighter corner? Does a destructive conflict then become inevitable? Not necessarily. If an interest is recognized and validated, very often the party expressing their difference will support a decision, even if it does not fully meet his or her request.

In such situations, it becomes important for the stakeholders to articulate their willingness to compromise. If a resolution is being facilitated by a mediator, that individual may even take time to ask for consent. The mediator may ask something such as, "Barb, we know the budget committee could not authorize the upgrade to the computer system that would allow you to work at home some days. However, are you willing to support the use of flex-time as an alternative to helping you meet your child-care needs?"

The three steps to becoming an interest bargainer are:

1. Always ask why.

2. Consider letting the other person have his or her way. Unconditional surrender may be in your best interest.

3. Find an alternative way to give the person what he or she wants.

Becoming an interest bargainer may be an advanced skill, but that does not mean it is overly difficult. In fact, a three year old demonstrated that she was well on her way to becoming a keen negotiator when her mother asked her to perform a small chore. The little girl suddenly became quite serious and said, "Mommy, I need a reason." Patiently, her mother responded with a reason for the request. The little girl thought for a moment, frowned and said, "But Mommy, I need a *good* reason."

SUMMARY

This book has provided you with a number of ways to handle difficult situations effectively. Awareness, willingness, logic and creativity, combined with good listening skills, will help you on your journey to becoming an effective manager and mediator of the variety of conflicts based on differences that are inevitable in today's homes and workplaces.

Be creative in your method of handling, managing and resolving differences. Don't allow your differences to result in a passionate debate in which you become driven by emotions, out of control. This condition makes you unable to think clearly or to use logical strategies to resolve your differences, which creates undue tension and breaks down communication. When communication breaks down, all parties walk away from the table feeling angry, hurt and defensive, while the issues of difference remain unresolved.

The most vital ingredient to resolving differences is your ability to negotiate. Remember that during the preconflict stage, different viewpoints can be most easily discussed, understood and ultimately incorporated into both your personal and professional life; when differences are addressed properly at their outset, you will successfully avoid nonproductive conflict. The seven principles to successful negotiation, combined with an effective persuasion strategy and consideration for the individual's true needs are your most powerful tools to help everyone involved in a dispute over differences to walk away feeling like a winner!

TOOL KIT FOR MANAGING DIFFERENCES

TOOL #1:
Problem Solving

When confronting a problem, these are some questions you should ask yourself:

1. Is this a symptom or a problem?

2. Is it related to a work need or a personal need?

3. Can we answer the following:

   Who   Where
   What   Why
   When   How

4. What results would we hope for? What change would we like to bring about?

5. Once we bring about this change, how will we evaluate whether it's working or not?

6. What's the worst thing that could happen if we make the wrong decision and mess this up?

7. If we make this change, what are the advantages?

8. If we make this change, what are the disadvantages?

9. Ultimately, will this be perceived as a "win-win" situation?

10. Always ask: "Who owns this problem?"
    "Who has control over this issue?"
    "Who will take action?"

11. Who will be affected or hurt by this problem?

12. Should I do something immediately?

13. Where did this problem come from (source)?

14. What action is going to be taken?

TOOL #2:
Seven Steps to Sell
Your Ideas to Others

1. Know exactly what it is that you want from the other person.

Visualize it clearly in terms of the other person's behavior or as so me other relevant outcome. Consider the total implications and results of this change in behavior or outcome, and make sure this is what you really want.

2. Be certain you're willing to pay for it.

You get very little from other people without paying some price for what you get. Can you afford the price? You'll probably have to pay in terms of the incentives the other person will need to sustain their new behaviors. Are you willing to accept changes in other areas to get what you want in this one?

3. Ask for it.

Too many people are either afraid to ask for what they really want, or they assume the other person somehow knows what it is. One of the biggest reasons we don't get what we want is that we never really ask for it.

4. Be specific.

Take that picture you created in Step 1 and share it *completely* and in living color with the other person.

5. Show the benefits.

Your idea must meet some self-interest for the other person, or it won't be accepted. You need a good answer to the question, "what's in it for me?" Document the specific advantages of your idea. Provide convincing supporting data. Know the other person's values, attitudes, and needs.

6. Overcome objections.

The best way to overcome an objection is to defuse it before it is raised. State it yourself as a valid criticism of your idea; then systematically and objectively dismantle it with the potential objector looking on as a spectator, not as a defender.

7. Thank the person.

Whether or not you succeed, thank the person for listening to you. If you get what you want, include a reassurance that the person will like the results. Leave him or her feeling good about you.

TOOL #3:
Negotiation Style Profile

This is a quick tool to help you discover your present style of negotiating.

Instructions: For each pair of bargaining characteristics, place an "x" on the scale where you believe your style is best represented.

Soft Bargaining Characteristics	Indicate Your Tendency	Hard Bargaining Characteristics
Participants are friends.	├────────┼────────┼────────┤	Participants are adversaries.
The goal is agreement.	├────────┼────────┼────────┤	The goal is victory.
Make concessions to cultivate the relationship.	├────────┼────────┼────────┤	Demand concessions as a condition of the relationship.
Be soft on the people and the problem.	├────────┼────────┼────────┤	Be hard on the problem and the people.

Trust others. ├────┼────┼────┤ Distrust others.

Change your ├────┼────┼────┤ Dig into your
position easily.   position.

Make offers. ├────┼────┼────┤ Make threats.

Disclose your ├────┼────┼────┤ Mislead as to
bottom line.   your bottom
                                          line.

Accept one- ├────┼────┼────┤ Demand one-
sided losses   sided gains as
to reach   the price of
agreement.   agreement.

Search for the ├────┼────┼────┤ Search for the
single answer: single answer:
the one *they*   the one *you*
will accept.   will accept.

Insist on ├────┼────┼────┤ Insist on your
agreement.   position.

Try to avoid ├────┼────┼────┤ Try to win
a contest   a contest
of wills.   of wills.

Yield to ├────┼────┼────┤ Apply pressure.
pressure.

HOW TO INTERPRET YOUR SCORES

Look at the "x's" on the scale. Where are they located?

Now, connect them up by drawing a line from one "x" to the next. Is your score indicating a preference for a "soft" or "hard" bargaining style?

Are you happy with this outcome? If not, start thinking about the questions and how you responded. Remember, you are in control. You can access either style—be conscious about your choices.

The Negotiation Process

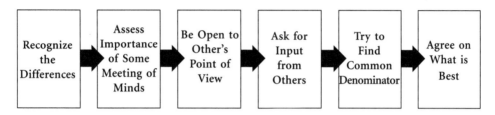

The skills you need to be a better negotiator are:

- Finely tuned listening skills
- Fact-finding skills

ACTION PLAN

What changes can you make to be a better negotiator?

_____

_____

_____

TOOL #4:
Six Steps to
Resolve Conflicts

STEP 1: **State the reasons for the meeting and lay the ground rules.**

You • State why you are meeting.

- Express your hope to resolve the conflict.
- Describe the six-step process
- Invite the other person to tell his or her side of the story.

STEP 2: **Each person states his/her side of the story while the others listens.**

Other • Tells his or her side of the story.
- You Listen actively.
- When the other is finished, restate what you have heard.
- Ask the other if you've heard correctly.
- Tell your side of the story.
- Both Emphasize facts.
- Avoid name calling.
- Describe behaviors, not motives.
- Use "I" rather than "You" statements.
- Listen to understand the others point of view.

STEP 3: **Express needs, hopes, and concerns.**

Both • State needs and hopes.
- Speculate on what might happen if the conflict is not resolved.

- Express what you have heard the other say.
- Try not to defend yourself: neither person is on trial.

STEP 4: Generate ideas towards a possible solution.

Both • Generate ideas
(brainstorm, make lists, ask what has worked for others).
- Each states a possible solution to the conflict.

STEP 5: Select a solution for implementation.

Both • Select a possible solution both can live with.
- Make a commitment to try and make it work.

STEP 6: Decide on follow-up.

Both • Set a time and place to meet again.
- Decide what would constitute success.
- Discuss the consequences of not following through.

TOOL #5:
Stating Complaints and
Requesting Change

A simple request

Example: "Jane I have a complaint. You are late to most of our group's meetings. I'd appreciate it if you would commit yourself to coming on time. Can you agree to that?"

Communicate friendly intentions and acknowledge your role.

Example: "Caroline, I appreciate your contributions to our group. (Pause) I do however have one complaint. You have not been completing patient flowsheets. I recognize that I haven't told you before that this upsets me, but I would like you to commit yourself to completing them by the end of the shift. Can you agree to that?"

DON'T DO

- Hinting
  Example: I thought it might be nice if you would be here when we start the meeting.

- Attacking
  Example: You are never here on time.

100

DO

- **Be assertive up front.**
  Example: We start here at 8:30.

- **State the complaint in behavioral terms.**
  Example: You are doing a great job, but it concerns me that you are frequently late.

- **Request directly that something be done.**
  Example: "Jane, we are rotating telephone duty. Each professional is asked to take a 30-minute duty once a month. Which day do you prefer?" (Have calendar in hand for person to write in their name.)

TOOL #6:
Influence Styles

Four approaches to influencing others are described below. For each description, indicate on the scale provided the degree to which you think the approach is characteristic of your own behavior in one-on-one influence encounters. It is not necessary that you compare the various approaches with one another. It is not intended that you rank the approaches relative to one another. You may for example judge your typical behavior to be high or low in any or all of the four approaches.

Approach #1

In influencing others I tend to rely heavily on logical arguments—getting the facts; marshalling the evidence. I do my homework carefully, and make sure that I leave no stone unturned in presenting all the facts and in developing counter arguments to anticipated points likely to be raised by the person I'm trying to influence.

```
 |     |     |     |     |     |     |     |     |     |     |
10    9     8     7     6     5     4     3     2     1     0
```
Very characteristic   Very uncharacteristic
of me   of me

Approach #2

In preparing to influence others I make very sure that I think through the possible hopes, values, and aspirations of the other person. I try to identify and articulate a common or shared vision of what the future might be like (for the individual, for others and/or for the organization) if the other person does what I am asking him/her to do. I often base my influence strategy on appeals to the other person's emotions, trying to kindle excitement about a better future which the other person may value for themselves or others or for the organization.

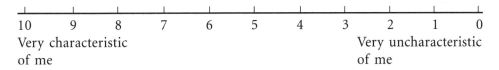

| 10 | 9 | 8 | 7 | 6 | 5 | 4 | 3 | 2 | 1 | 0 |

Very characteristic
of me   Very uncharacteristic
                                                 of me

Approach #3

In influencing others I make very sure to let the other person realize that I want his/her input and value his/her contribution. I don't push my point of view—but rather spend a lot of time drawing the other person out. I don't rush decisions—but let the other person know that there is plenty of time for us to explore one another's views before any decision needs to be made. I try to encourage the other person's participation in any decision in order to build his/her commitment.

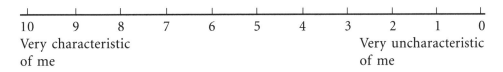

| 10 | 9 | 8 | 7 | 6 | 5 | 4 | 3 | 2 | 1 | 0 |

Very characteristic
of me   Very uncharacteristic
                                                 of me

Approach #4

In influencing others I don't hesitate to rely on my status or formal authority to get my way. I also feel that both praise and criticism and the offering of rewards or implying the possibility of penalties is a legitimate and often necessary approach in accomplishing one's personal and/or organizational goals.

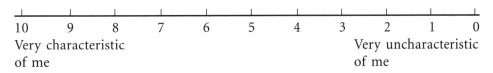

| 10 | 9 | 8 | 7 | 6 | 5 | 4 | 3 | 2 | 1 | 0 |

Very characteristic
of me   Very uncharacteristic
                                                 of me

Draw your influence profile below.

	10			
	9			
	8			
	7			
	6			
	5			
	4			
	3			
	2			
	1			
	0			

Approach #1: Logical Persuasion

Approach #2: Common Vision

Approach #3: Participation & Trust

Approach #4: Power

TOOL #7:
Problem Solving Using
Force-Field Analysis

This tool is a simple tool to use. This tool forces you to think logically about how to solve your dilemma. The method helps you identify and deal with the forces that assist or obstruct a change you want to make. The forces that help you achieve the change are called driving forces, and the forces opposed are called restraining forces. This tool only takes a few minutes. Here's how to use it:

STEP 1: Draw a force-field chart (a large "T").

STEP 2: Write the current situation at the top center of the chart.

STEP 3: Write the desired situation at the top right of the chart.

STEP 4: Brainstorm for driving forces (pushing toward what you want) and enter them on the left side of the chart.

STEP 5: Brainstorm for restraining forces (preventing you from getting what you want) and enter them on the right side of the chart.

STEP 6: Discuss the chart and determine which forces could be altered to increase the chances of success.

STEP 7: Decide whether your solution is doable. If it is, make a list of action items to alter the forces. If it isn't develop another solution.

Current Situation	What You Want
(−)	(+)

TOOL #8:
Life's Little Annoyances

ost personal dilemmas occur as a result of procrastinating. Here's a simple exercise to help you frame and resolve your dilemma. Just follow the boxes.

STEP 1: Think about the thing that is "bugging" you the most right now. Record it in Box 1.

Box 1

STEP 2: Give yourself 30 second. Think of everything you can do to resolve or rid this "thing" or situation; record your answers in Box 2.

Box 2

STEP 3: Now, write a description of what it would be like to be rid of this situation in Box 3.

Box 3

STEP 4: Now you are ready to take some action. Formulate a strategy to rid this "thing" or situation and record it in Box 4.

Box 4

If you enjoyed this book. Please write or call for
our catalog:

CRISP
PUBLICATIONS

1200 Hamilton Court
Menlo Park, CA 94025
1 (800) 442–7477
FAX (415) 323–5800